OBJECTS IN MIRROR

objects in mirror
n. w. downs

Querencia Press – Chicago IL

QUERENCIA PRESS

© Copyright 2024
N.W. Downs

All Rights Reserved

No reproduction, copy or transmission of this publication may be made without written permission.
No paragraph of this publication may be reproduced, copied, or transmitted save with the written permission of the author.

Any person who commits any unauthorized act in relation to this publication may be liable to criminal prosecution and civil claims for damages.

ISBN 978 1 959118 97 8

www.querenciapress.com

First Published in 2024

**Querencia Press, LLC
Chicago IL**

Printed & Bound in the United States of America

*make me want what i want
another wayward son
waiting on oblivion*

- anaïs mitchell, "young man in america"

for Durango, who is still alive

CONTENTS

COYOTE 13
CLOSE AS I COULD GET TO JACKSONVILLE, FLORIDA 14
SQUAM LAKE 16
RADIO NOISES...17
IN NEW YORK 19
SOMETHING LIKE MARCELLA 21
YOUR FLAG DECAL WON'T GET YOU INTO HEAVEN
ANYMORE...23
THE DIFFERENCE BETWEEN CALLING YOU "MOM" AND
CALLING YOU "MA" 25
PORTLAND, ME → PORTLAND, OR...27
RACHAEL 29
TROLLEY PROBLEMS 32
IN MASSACHUSETTS 33
DURANGO 35
FIRST YEAR WITH G 37
IN HENRY FORD'S AMERICA 38
WHEN I SAY MY HANDS HAVE NEVER BEEN EMPTIER I
MEAN.. 41
NOT TO WORRY 42
IN ILLINOIS.. 44
TWO NATIONS ARE IN THY WOMB..46
HARVEST TIME..48
DRIP...49
DON'T BE A STRANGER...51

IN KENTUCKY	53
WHERE R U GOING ?	54
WHAT WE TALK ABOUT WHEN WE TALK ABOUT WAYLON JENNINGS	55
CROSSING THE MISSISSIPPI	58
NEW GUARD	60
ROAD KILL	61
POEM 29	64
IN WISCONSIN	65
ROUTE 44 CHERRY LIMEADE	67
END OF LIFE	68
ALL THE DOGS ARE DIFFERENT NOW	69
1/7/2020	71

COYOTE

my mom's mom dies. it's simple.
some guy t-boned some other guy
into the guardrail at 118 & locust
maybe five or six years ago,
spat soot and all but stopped
afternoon school traffic.
endless faces for my grief to wear.
endless faces.
people from the suburbs
are a difficult breed.
my sister told me what happened
to stella's new foal
over a bowl of fettuccine
in one of three local olive gardens.
most of what you have to know
you see in the rearview
or out at the edge of the yard
near dusk, between watered-down
rosebushes and those woods.
in reverse they seem as tall
as giants, thousand branches
braced black against evening.
coming in and washing my feet
in the pink upstairs bathtub—
what's this memory? whose?
my mom's mom dies and it's simple.
she'll die next. then me.

CLOSE AS I COULD GET TO JACKSONVILLE, FLORIDA

your buddy posts a video of you hanging halfway out the passenger seat of a shimmer-dark sedan. white as a sand dune. i know it's you 'cause i know it's you.

forget what mom says when she gets sad. house can't hold all it. cold up here, that's all, we think of you shiny on the highway shoulder and get jealous.

last week they took the wal-mart down on account of everybody moving away. couple of the guys met near the bank to watch the first hit. landed like a crow in a window.

if i ever get my own plot of land, i'm going to fill it so full of magnolia trees they choke. hasn't happened yet, mostly stoops and sills. holding out.

you'll come back. i don't mean home. i mean to me, like this, that sweat and shoulder.

even to the cold. i can't bring myself down there, man, i can't take the sun. you know how it gets up north. you know the only highways we take run east to west.

you unfold from the car and land on the pavement. looks white-hot, get up, are you choking on your joy or your tongue down there? are you eating well?

forget what mom says when she says your name. don't mean it.

come visit. get off the ground. steal the car. your buddy empties a beer on your head, not unkind but it's strange, it's a language i don't speak. you stayed good and quiet getting baptized as a baby. not now,

howling all over the place somewhere farther south i've ever been. i pray for you. not to god. not to that god.

said when one of the big walls came down it raised so much dust the crew had to call the rest of the day off. where's it come from? everything bone-pale, want to hit it all real hard. see what stirs up.

SQUAM LAKE

from the wide porch of her ex-husband's summer home
we watched rachel throw the dust that was left of him
down into the stone beach's thin water, settling velvet
on the splintered rock. on the drive down from
the mountains we listened to the news and the old shepherd
left his nose on every window. and rachel
cut her hair real short, threw away his clothes,
stayed in the summer home even when the lake
iced over, rocker thumping on the porch, firelit.
this mythology will not falter. we're old as the hills.
our men in their shallow water freeze and flood
and wreck themselves into a stupor on the dock.
it's not a circle, it's something worse. once i saw
something we don't talk about on the bottom of the lake,
it was a hot one and we were all seeing things
that weren't there. you said you didn't,
but i know you stayed under too long
the last time the tow tube threw you,
and i know you didn't get back on after that.
wasn't too much later rachel tried to move away,
got pulled back, doing her time now
serving as sentry, then who knows.
maybe she'll try again. if i visit her
i'll call you. i'll let you know.

RADIO NOISES

not everyone knows how they'll die, but i do. explained it real clear while you drove me north my first year at college, burning the highway up. those years are hard to remember, they smudge out 'round the edges. i was mostly pain between girl and man. all that skin to be pulled back. you had a thing for hank senior, liked how he sounded singing from the driver's side speaker of your busted up toyota. i was sure i'd die in a car and you said lots of guys die in cars, don't mean anything. you were born in massachusetts and couldn't play the guitar for shit or else you may have been something. i was born in massachusetts and couldn't play the guitar for shit, guess anyone could about tell by looking. don't matter, dad taught us local radio stations better than our own blood, we knew where to find johnny & george and we knew how to get home. my last year of school i drove you up route 1 into maine and you said those old guys on the radio sure have soft voices. i'm on the other side of a few things now, no clue how i got here or which station to set the radio on. when i came home with a new name you told me waylon jennings named his son after a gun and if you weren't a coward you'd do the same. you weren't kind to me but i think you wanted to be. who else had done it, the only party trick anyone cared to see, the old bait and switch. the rabbit leaves the hat, the dove leaves the sleeve, the car cranks itself open like an accordion and lets the body out for one last drive down the highway with the old boys and their sons gone crazy against the windshield, pedal on the floor fit to snap.

IN NEW YORK

man and boy
in the car behind us.

we got caught up
in the school rush,

'bout died laughing
at the rearview

watching them
knuckle-deep

in their two
matching noses.

standstill traffic,
hot as hell.

eating off their hands
together. audience

be damned.
wasn't i a good

brother to you?
didn't we make

it to mom's house
before the rain

started, the way
i said we would?

isn't every family
kind to each other

in some way?

SOMETHING LIKE MARCELLA

whatever it takes, do not
read this one aloud. when the
   neighbor died
mom didn't talk about it. this week
i dreamt of a house in the night
in a field somewhere in kentucky,
so far back up the bloodline it hits the
   heart,
three windows in the west wall
glassy-facing some purple nothing.
no car in the long cracked drive
and the answering machine
   promised
can't get stars like this any'ere else.
i don't remember my dad's ma's first
   name:
that's how many generations it takes.
out and out past scrubby grass
something like a mountain was
   eating the stars
one by one, heavy in the dark and not
   in a hurry.
when mom calls me a blindspotter
she means i can keep a secret. like
a crocheted blanket in the back of an
   ambulance.
she was old, anyways, and the
   flashing lights
so pretty on my bedroom ceiling.

i could measure the country with the
    growing distance between us:
she's pulling away through
    yellownight
towards the big house and i am
where i have been, in bed
with my eyes open.

YOUR FLAG DECAL WON'T GET YOU INTO HEAVEN ANYMORE

the summer you got thrown from the
   tow tube
a family of bats moved into our
   cabin.
they put up the nights
caterwauling against the rafters.
jacob's first wife chased after them
   with a broom, no luck,
i hid and you swore
you heard them say my name.
i can live without the guilt,
i can live well without it.
people want to be kind to each other
   but there's us in the way.
in the dark i wanted you, it was
   mostly senseless,
i was mostly afraid.
i kept thinking: *the next bat i hear, i'll*
   ask him to come into bed with me.
and the night would be so quiet.
jacob's first wife returned to the big
   house,
her boot laces skittering through
   leaves and low brush.
what have i done with these hands?
   my brother is cruel to me and i
   am cruel to him.

in the dark he never moved closer
and he never pulled away.
i could measure the country with the
    distance between us,
steady and good, i could build a
    house with it
in the middle of kentucky, a sturdy,
    good house,
with a long driveway, and her
    curtains all opened up to big sky.

THE DIFFERENCE BETWEEN CALLING YOU "MOM" AND CALLING YOU "MA"

is one of them's not your name

sorry for renaming myself
on your new kitchen floor

and sorry for suggesting
that your children may be evidence

that there are more paths
through girlhood than there are girls

the way there are more gunshots
than victims not everyone

makes it out of the
bloodbath innocent

and though it's true i was not
a boy when i was supposed to be

wasn't i something close to it
the way a deer in the corner

of an eye is something
close to a deer or

another woman's son is something
closer to your own than your own

mom if i'm good for anything
it's shaving names down

to stubble clipped and toothless
unrecognizing the form

and mounting its head
above the door i could push

glass eyes into the name
i don't call you

hold my palm open on its dead
feathery nose know it won't bite

know it won't ask me to stay
mom the list of things i want

is actually so short
but none of it is simple

anyways if i know
anything it's that

changing a name
is one thing but

cleaning the bones
is another

PORTLAND, ME → PORTLAND, OR

7am on the chicago beach   unlike back east
it goes straight down   unlike back east
there's no salt
                        i know who cut
   the heartstrings i watched the bastard do it
i wasn't the one holding the gun
but i never told him not to shoot
                              lately
     it's all hollering and heartache
    remember the winter the neighbor had to
drive us home   can't remember where
mom was   the only station coming
             through was playing pianos
      just sort of swirling in the blizzard
brother brother you said your first bad word
when we made it home without a house key
         spent the night on the neighbor's couch
     crocheted afghans
   and oyster crackers in lentil soup
after lights-out we had our heads between glass
  and lace watching it snow down and you were
  saying your new word over and over until it
  softened into sugar and smoke on the back of
  your tongue
        the city beach has needles in the sand
     almost stepped on one

                        on the train home
a man explains what blood from a dead body is
good for   three years ago
         i got in my car to drive to oregon
     you know some things about unfinished
business   you were kind
as a child
 in ways you didn't understand and couldn't
  follow through on   left the
         racecars in the backyard
    through three rainstorms
they sank into the mud
                  never pulled them up
before we moved away
  i spent a summer breaking toes on a bumper
        only half-buried in the dirt
hobbling around the yard me and the damn car
and your red knees

RACHAEL

the year i stopped smoking cigarettes
was a bad one.
jacob's second wife called to tell us
she'd found a house in the swiss alps—
or was it just a view of them?—
and likely would die there
before she dreamt of coming back
to where her husband couldn't keep the pigs alive
and most of the rivers
were roads for four months out of the year.
and i, genetically insane
or else crazy in some less interesting
but more damning way i couldn't hold
my finger still enough to put it on,
gave up on the guitar
and the explanations and took to making small talk
with the man in 204 who smokes menthols
and doesn't remember the vietnam war
but says it doesn't matter,
his hands don't know that.
the year i stopped smoking cigarettes
i forgot every synonym for panic
and listened to merle haggard
until the floorboards bled
red mud all the way up to the knee,
ruining the sheets.
and every day at eight
a woman in a white car parked in the cemetery
outside my apartment window
to let her poodle shit between the headstones.

the year i stopped smoking cigarettes
i turned three years clean of the east coast
and four clean of alcohol
if you don't count a few nights here and there
where the dog died or the vietnam war
felt closer than it really was.
and in october, jacob's second wife
called to tell us her swiss lover
had found something younger than she was
and she was coming home,
or she was packing her bags
and there wasn't anywhere else
she knew all the highway exits,
so might as well. and last
i heard from home was my mom
said she'd have called it all years back
if anyone'd believed her.
would take me about sixteen hours
of solid driving
to recognize my own hands again.
not counting smoke stops, because.
oh, and i saw god once,
on a wednesday after my shift.
he was on the other sidewalk
leaving blue clouds behind
like an airplane in crisis.
it was one of those nights without any wind,
bizarre in the windy city,

the trees were all rigid spindles
lashed to the ceiling
sort of dangerous.
like jacob's second wife
when she called us from the airport
but didn't say anything.
the phone's speaker picked up
a final boarding call
from inside the plane
or outside of it.

TROLLEY PROBLEMS

mom taught me to drive. there are cars and dogs on the road, she said. hit the dog every time. two years later i drove north, and a semi drove into the rottweiler back home. she died on the driveway. you said someone got out of the cab and he was playing that van zandt song you hate, you said he had a rose tattooed on his forehead and helped you wrap the dog in blankets. i'm always taking your word for things but i heard you weren't there, i heard you'd been gone a month at that point. didn't show face again for another three and when you did you had a dent in your bumper, blamed a lightpost for it. you stole mom's picnic blanket ten years ago, used to keep it in your backseat, but i guess it walked off at some point. when you told me about the guy with the rose you weren't angry, and you were angry about most things. said he made an honest show of himself, said he was torn up and cried some. but don't we gotta make choices, you said, and fast. maybe he was tired or scared or high. maybe the dog was moving so fast, after a squirrel or a turkey in the long strand of unclaimed land across the street. she was mom's favorite. she had a strong head and big soft paws, she knew her name and answered to it.

IN MASSACHUSETTS

men in still water
and waders waiting

for the bogs to flood up.
only to the ankle now,

but it's something.
we ate only cranberry

ice cream that summer,
made ourselves sick

sweating it out
in the rushed breeze

of route 6 traffic pulling
at us like rip sand

while the farmers were
getting ready to harvest.

you could have
taken that job

standing down in the red
with the rest of them,

you could have been
tall and jagged,

our mom's little
paul bunyan in your

big boots and cap.
ankle deep in still

water, a version
of you reflecting,

and his hands
full of berries.

DURANGO

one of the labradors we raised and gave away comes
    home ten years later, old and fat and as familiar
    as a hurricane in wisconsin.
they say things change but they don't know the half of it.
when my sadness was easy, it was lilac and peat,
and once lightning struck the tree in the backyard while
    we stood under it together,
this dog and i. until then i had not heard a noise like
    that.
i carried him into the house. now
he is there again but i am not, i am in my ten years and
    i have nothing in my hands.
is it better to be there at the end or the beginning?
i carried him into the house with my heart all caught up
    in cymbals.
i carried him into the house and he is old now,
he is going to die the way dogs do,
wreathed in flowers and flannels.
love in dog years does not stretch thin, he'll crack the
    tree in half on the first go, he'll bring the roof down
    with him.
is it more forgivable to leave or to come back? i was
    fifteen once and i haven't recovered.
in a video on an old camera i find him learning to howl
    at turkeys through the front window,
his golden dust mite halo and big feet.
tonight there is a swarm of gnats trapped on the
    elevated train, frenzied under the fluorescents.

my sister sends a photo of the dog in our mom's house
    and he is in my hands again. somewhere there's a
    plane already off the ground
and i'm supposed to be on it. the gnats rally in their blue
    buzz.
i am as kind as i was ten years ago, and the dog is still
    alive.

FIRST YEAR WITH G

skinning knuckles of ginger at the kitchen counter, persuading gnocchi. we drip balsamic vinegar onto slices of pizza made without cheese. curry splatters onto my new white shirt. i measure three cups of flour into a takeaway container. orange peels everywhere, my thumb stays stained. ice water. kimchi jjigae four nights in a row. she likes her cookies soft, i like mine crusty. we hide mushrooms in crepes and dumplings. we eat the last of her sibling's dino nuggets. those sweet potatoes. endless tea, always scrubbing the cups. my knuckles red in the sink, dishrag wrung and wrung. olive and spinach hand pies from the bakery on the corner, oil on chin. italian ice: mango, guava, coconut, peach. we don't make it through the menu in our first year, then april resets. crystals in a paper cup. sucking the plastic spoon. ready to try again.

IN HENRY FORD'S AMERICA

i am waiting for a test that can determine whether some people are truly incapable of love. while i wait, i am so helpful.

that old passenger van spun out on christmas eve, tire tracks on the white highway and bones all around. good church shoes on the median. low sky.

see, nobody writes poems anymore because we're too busy fixing the cars.

on april 27, 2019, the local power plant's cooling towers were detonated after only six years of use. boats with eyes crowding mount hope bay and cars all down the riverfront. you can't tell but i didn't start speaking until fifteen. you can't tell but i am doing my best.

lover wants me to speak clearly but it's shameful. can't afford new brakes, tires gone bald, driver's side fender taped onto the frame. bite marks in the steering wheel from god knows what. busted power windows, no air.

when the ten-passenger van broke down for good we bought a winstar with less than two years left on the road. i learned to circle parking lots in a blue toyota with a silver hood, cooling towers spitting steam on the other side of town.

you gotta stop acting like you're the only one doing this for the first time, a friend in providence said as i drove him down the steep hill from the east side. *none of us have been men before.*

what am i without the car, baby, can't pick you up from the airport or take the dog to the vet, can't make off to wisconsin if we both need some fresh air for once, can't finish that long haul west.

my sister met the man she'd later marry drag racing open jeeps down country back roads with no street lights for miles. they both swear they've seen ghosts near the reservoir and wouldn't have made it home if they'd stopped the car.

my first car took me to new hampshire. she took me to maine. she took me to new york city and the galilee beach and she made a one-way trip through pennsylvania and endless ohio just to break metal on chicago's south side.

i thought i knew a few things about love, none of the big stuff, but enough to go on. like how to memorize an address, how to parallel park on the first try, how to keep the backseat clean and have blankets and jumper cables in the trunk.

my mom's mom dies and she drives the van home as a keepsake. when dad answers the phone he says *how's that car holding up?*

they've got their own vanishing hitchhiker back home, some tall guy in a red jacket. easy enough, you gotta drive on without stopping to offer him a ride. plenty of folks can't even do that—can't say i don't understand.

our neighbor died before i was tall enough to ride in the passenger seat, nobody too torn up until his daughter came to move his white sedan from the driveway over a year later. couldn't get it to start, thing sat dead in the cracking heat just bone-still. watched dad watching from the window, one hand working the doorknob back and forth.

WHEN I SAY MY HANDS HAVE NEVER BEEN EMPTIER I MEAN

she wants to replace the center console
with our fingers. skokie sky stretches
out further than in the city, night
on the ground but the light holds on.
her bedroom window faces
a bedroom window, i roll mine down
and the song rushes in between the teeth.
what if heaven's a car dealership at dusk,
too bright? where am i going? where are you?
with one exception, my people
have always taken their time dying, wasted
away the little hours going on and on.
throw me in the lake, lover. the millstone.
even in the purple brushstrokes
out at the edge of evening, i feel
something chewing furiously, even
in the presence of the pretty secrets
we've trapped in the center console.
it's not true my mom's mom will finish dying
when she returns to the big house.
it happens much sooner than that,
or much later. lover rewinds the tape
and we get back on the highway. skyline
silvering ahead. i know you wish
i would cry more, lover, but
someone has to drive. someone
has to keep an eye on the road
or it gets away.

NOT TO WORRY

doesn't someone have to drive and carry and shovel and plan and lift and pay and be the first one in the last one out doesn't someone have to cook and remember and protect and make the bed answer the phone carry the groceries in from the car so forget kindnesses aren't i useful aren't i workhorse stuff baby don't i only let you touch the thick skin and by now don't you know someone's gotta be the one to push and push and push and push and push and push and push and push and push and won't i make it okay baby don't i have to doesn't someone and either way baby isn't the dream just work and can't i work baby forget

the niceties aren't i a
goddamn trooper aren't
i stubborn enough to
march it out with a bad
leg and a rotten tooth
weather be damned out
there in the mud just
pushing and sweating
and pushing

IN ILLINOIS

mailman halts outside
the christmas house,

something near to
reverence. offers a

long whistle, he says
when i get my house

*i'll be the biggest santa
on the block. that's*

*the dream. biggest
santa on the block.*

he's only got one
glove on, one half

of his face isn't
shaped like the other.

he says *people gonna
talk about me.*

*when i get my house
they won't be able*

to shut up. the christmas
house has a button

on the mailbox
that'll sing you a song

but when he pushes it
nothing happens.

TWO NATIONS ARE IN THY WOMB

mom doesn't remember which of us came first but she hopes it was you. in the bar under the motel 6 you bought me a whiskey. half of the parking lot was in massachusetts and the other half wasn't. i had a habit of walking out of step with you, too far behind.

you're not special, shooter, everyone wants more time with the tulip trees than they get. i know you're worried the dead guys on the radio never felt the way you do. i know it gets worse, shooter, nobody knows this better than i do.

you're my older brother. you're my younger brother. you're a stranger i met once on a front lawn in kentucky.

on a napkin you listed the things you thought were waiting for you down south. the glasses sweat all over it, no matter, they'd wait. we disagreed on where the state line landed by about thirty feet. i have a clear memory of your heel in my hand.

you're one of two sons. you're one of seven daughters. if you'd been born at all mom would call you a miracle, she'd dress you in boots and heavy magnolias.

every true thing you've told me you've said on the phone or in the car. if it's true objects in the mirror are closer than they appear then we both have some fixing up to do. i drove a steak knife half an inch into your forearm fifteen years ago, you stole my seat at the table every time.

what i feel for you isn't love, shooter. you bought me a drink but that doesn't forgive anything. we both left boxes of shit behind in massachusetts and agree that going back for them would kill us.

the year your car broke down i drove you everywhere, took us to the bar so you could buy me a drink for my birthday. driving slow circles in the parking lot, practicing our exodus.

you're an american but i'm the second-youngest child, my country learned all its tricks before i woke up. sorry about the time i used your good pocketknife to carve roads in the dirt, i didn't know about the plowshares, i didn't know the birthright was mine.

it's true i drove west alone. it's true mom gave birth to one daughter after another. it's true i can't be the one to break her curse.

cut it out, you said. *making me dizzy in these fucking circles.* and anyways it looked like rain so i drove us back for one more summer in her house. when my nation goes to war we will be with pruning hooks. my people have come up from the dirt.

when you finally went south you left your boots behind, the only thing of yours i can't wear. you're mine.

you're me. you're the father and the son and the habits they can't break. you're god, shooter. you're just some guy with a gun.

HARVEST TIME

word from home is dad's softening up
boiling back down to
who he probably was
before we knew him
word from home is
he's looking at tickets to chicago

                                              my favorite part of the city is
                             just off the south-bound red line tracks
                                   between belmont and fullerton
                                         someone's put a sign
                                           up in their bedroom window
                                                         it says

                       where r
                       u going
                       ?

dad had a friend who died of
alzheimer's he was forty-four he was
catatonic

.

DRIP

tornado sirens start back up
in the diner we put on
a fresh pot of coffee
stand at the window watching
the gauze stretch green
between the trees
above north broadway
it's april it's chicago
it's as simple as it gets
i'm out of quarters for laundry
and the grocery bag's
handle gave way yesterday
my old shitbox
finally broke down
and left me here
wiping vinyl booths
under the green and
perpetually missing the bus
soon i'll have been
three years in this place
soon i'll be twenty-five
and my hands have
never been emptier
i let my good boots crack and
not even the tornado touches
down we have to clear the plates
and sweep up walk home dry
you'd be humiliated if you knew
there are no hurricanes

in the city only tornado
warnings empty promises no
twister no oz
no nothing
if i caught a greyhound
further west would you
ride with me
just to fill the space
there's so much of it out here
not a trick this time i swear
you wouldn't have to talk
i wouldn't ask you to stay

DON'T BE A STRANGER

be quiet and
listen. it's the first day of summer,
she and i are cottonmouthed at the ice cream
    parlor on southport
and time is still moving through the tall grass
flattening spring's green behind us.
in love someone is always leaving. ask me the
    question again and i won't lie
this time: it's me, it's me. my best
is not as good as hers. in the graveyard
the grass is already breaking itself in yellow half,
    too soon.
i thought we had the summer still, her lozenges
    and baskets of fruit
spread untouched across the blanket.
i got to talking about a new car and she got wise,
that's curtains for caution. in love someone is
    always lonely.
over and over i walked down this street years ago,
    i didn't imagine anything.
the tall grass bows. to lie bellydown in the dirt
in the garden again, before all of this,
when all things existed but i had named only a
    few of them.
in love someone's parents are always to blame.
she holds me like one of her soft animals. she
    comforts me
in a language she knows i don't speak.
there is a summer in which i can be kind forever
and the grass grows and grows.

there is a summer in which i have all the money
    we need
and the nights are cool. i love her there.
we understand each other easily and the elevated
    train
is moved three blocks south so we can sit with our
    ice creams
and hear one another talk. in love
someone is always too hungry. i tell the truth
but the train passes overhead,
i apologize in a language she can't hear.
and time is still moving through the dying grass
    towards itself,
or away from itself,
so patient and so familiar.

IN KENTUCKY

old boy shaped all
dirt thin & haired

like a rat. quit menthols
but carries a light.

one yellow tooth.
the others white white.

neck broken backwards
checkin fer storms.

crow's feet stretch
far enough to snap,

windnumb tears
in the canyon.

god made this.
on purpose.

family's another word
for hunger.

could probably fit
both his shoulders

in my mouth,
gnawing bone.

WHERE R U GOING ?

here's the yellow spider who lived a summer on the back fence. dad named it after his brother, who was not dead then and is not now. he is alive and well in a shotgun house in louisville, overfeeding the cat and meeting the old boys at the sports bar. *the things you do in remembrance of me are killing me.* i stopped making memories a few years ago, out of places to put them. in my heels i remember my cousin on the rock beach, swimming out too far past the buoys, and mud daubers on the picnic blanket. in my hands i remember every dirt, and the old dog's rough collar.

WHAT WE TALK ABOUT WHEN WE TALK ABOUT WAYLON JENNINGS

somewhere in kansas you change your mind and start talking again. this is what it's like to share a house with a bigger sadder man:

not enough pain relief to go around. by now we know that anything we can't see from the bus windows

exists only in the future, the future that clicks from before to behind in a fraction of a second. keeps leaving us alone with the empty present. you say you wish i'd packed the guitar instead of giving it away in chicago,

no matter i hadn't learned to play. it's the principle of the thing to you.

man, there's fuck all out here, you say. testing the silence. i don't know about you, but i hope it won't hold your weight.

how do i tell you that all of my nightmares happen in the middle of the country? you, who dream in east-coast technicolor and don't know that out on the plains folks have to wait for permission to speak.

how do i tell you that i know things you don't? you, who wore all of my clothes first and took the greyhound west with me just to turn around and risk it on a plane back home to where mom's painting the living room roadkill-pink for the second time. if it weren't for me you wouldn't be the favorite

son, you wouldn't win a birthright. our sisters grew up and now we can't remember their names.

to be a son is to hold the gun. the bullet's in your name but you never knew where to point it, we're halfway

through kansas and i'm making some suggestions. miles out my window i can see you'll run away, too. it's the principle of the thing.

got your waylon & willie tape in my backpack, it's the only thing i've ever stolen from you and you won't see it again. shoot the bus up, man, take us out. a crime's only as deadly as the shooter's mother

and i'll take the last hit, i'll help you all the way. you, who take things real personal, who can't play the guitar either

and won't try now, what do you have left to teach me? yellow kansas is mine, i can see in your hands

you've never thought of it that way before. you'll never make it west of the mississippi after this. we can both see it out the window:

the future, the sons' country divided, paint wet on the living room walls.

if mom had named me i bet it would have been something awful. if she had it her way we'd be doctors, or lawyers. none of this cowboy shit. too late now, she'd have us get off the bus

and walk home together.

CROSSING THE MISSISSIPPI

the passenger seat is empty and my sisters are all back east. far as i can tell, there's only one unforgivable sin and it's the one i couldn't live without. clean from cigarettes now, took a while and my hands still shake. o god. the highway does not stop, i just got off. sisters, when i say i want to go home i mean my hands have never been emptier. when i say my hands have never been emptier i mean i miss you. am i a man or an american first? each has half of me in its stomach and is still so hungry. neither has kept its promises. sisters, you have a brother now but i don't. where will i go for violence? when i changed my name the clerk registered me in the military draft. everywhere there's a man, there's america, there's a gun, there's a car wearing itself out on a highway. my country promised i could have the body i want so long as i wear it like a weapon, and what did the coyote teach us when we were young? don't we know best about tooth and claw? only one of us can cross this river, sisters, only one of us can start the tape over again. this is the difference between the motherland and everywhere else. this is the difference between a child and a childhood. sorry i unsistered myself the way that i did, can't wring the violence out of my hands, can't walk softly. don't you know the only thing i wanted was to be a brother to you? none of this caution, i've had half a foot in the river my whole life. trying to figure out how to cross it without leaving you behind. sisters, the violence ends. when the coyote dies i will be there with flowers. when the river dries i will walk back to you. it's the cigarettes, sisters, it's that old white sedan. if i had a brother he'd talk sense into me but i don't. alone at the mississippi, we all know i'll cross it. look down into the water. didn't the atlantic prepare us for this? isn't this sin just a small one, just a soft one? some things are survivable. you come up on the other side, shake off, walk on alone.

NEW GUARD

last year in the fall
my second-oldest sister had a son
depending on how you look at it
he's the first son born
in too many generations
of bringing husbands in
and sending daughters out
depending on how you look at it
he'll save us all
so small this prized child
proof we're not forgotten
proof we can be forgiven
that's just how hayseeds
worship you give us one
good thing and we invent
god every time

ROAD KILL

the year i stopped smoking cigarettes
i moved into an apartment
on magnolia avenue it's ironic
it's something close to good and
i'm almost old enough now to admit
your house was a home ma
not mine but someone's way before us
we could feel them in the walls sometimes
we knew they had been loved there
the way a pitted gum feels
after the tooth has been pulled
numb and swollen with tenderness
for something that's not coming back
which may be why once
as a child i saw the devil
bleed out of the television
into your half-painted living room
the one with the bay window facing
out over route 6 where the wild turkeys
died in the worst way flattened one
at a time crossing from our lawn
where we fed them dry oatmeal
to the strand of thin woods
where they did the things turkeys do
when people aren't looking like
sleeping i think and singing
heavy treebranch songs and ma
between the turkeys and dogs
and rabbits and fish i wager

more things died in your house
than lived it's gotta wear you down
being out there in the backwater
nothing like the city apartment
where you slept so close
to the elevated train you could
reach out and touch it but didn't
too sensible as a girl you knew
life was terrible and would get worse
with or without you
ma how'd you end up living
in a town without a laundromat
just cow shit and packies
how'd you end up raising
all those daughters on your own
statistically it's not so bad
you only lost one the turkeys
did much worse than that
one year they all died
and another all but two
don't take it too hard ma
didn't i sneak around too quietly
at night always jumping you
clean from your skin and
isn't some of the sadness
gone from your house now
when your ma died
you were in the room
and i think we both know

that pattern ends here
you'll have to haunt the house ma
you can't haunt me
when you moved out of the city
did you see it going this way
or did you think every house
out in the boondocks had a mouth
full of tulip trees six daughters
strong on a swingset and a porch
with a trellis growing morning
glories so thick you couldn't
pull them apart if you tried
and the first night you saw a coyote
make off with a poult in its mouth
did it change anything or did
you buckle up and soldier on
making the best of it tearing
the old fence down and
building it back up
taller and sturdier
devils be damned

POEM 29

if i change my name,
refuse to forgive me. say
i've done nothing wrong.

IN WISCONSIN

in the room with the doll
carousels he sits heavily

on a bench beside his
two pink daughters. he

says *girls this is what*
it's like to have a dream

and make it happen. he
is using his church voice.

his kneeling voice. *girls*
imagine making something.

he's wearing a t-shirt from
john prine's last world tour

and a hat from the cheese
castle. some of the dolls

are riding doll horses
and one is riding a horse-

shaped man. he's close
to tears, hands open on his lap.

the dolls circle to broken
organ music. he says

*oh, my god, girls. don't you
see them? look. look.*

ROUTE 44 CHERRY LIMEADE

the colorado border   a porch and space for a chair

    and a window for the cat   a room with a braided

    rug   paintbrushes bleeding blue on the bench

a hand smaller than mine   a yellow morning

for the cat not to die   perfectly ripe peaches for three

    months straight   the tree   good sleep

one week of heavy heavy rain   my brother's boots

three small cups of tea   three mouths   the

    quilt my mom's mom made six years ago   put back together

or taken apart   or put back together

END OF LIFE

or a circle,
or the note says
i never loved you either
and
i forgive us

this is natural

i hope it's like a blanket
i hope you forget about me first
and quickly

don't have to carry my bones with your own
down the trail to the lake
i hope it's a trail to the lake

on the way up from florida
we listen to rap music
my sister's new dog falls asleep on my lap

we pass trailer parks and diners
and a statue of a little deer
with her head lowered into the tall grass
paint balding away from the spot
just between her shoulders

ALL THE DOGS ARE DIFFERENT NOW

and last i heard of the house on the lake was
it got bought up by a family from buffalo,
out-of-towners with a red truck and two
blond boys. i've known so many men and
none of them have been kind to me without
disguising it as something else.

my mom's mom had a wooden rocking
horse at the top of the stairs for many years,
spooking us silly in the blue dark. it's in my
sister's house in virginia now, toothless
and dwarfed by her new doberman's huge
feet and mouth.

either i am capable of love or i am not. it's
true i saw the devil once. it's true i gave up
on the guitar and wrecked my first car
trying to get away from a man in chicago.
most everything else is peripheral, smudgy
in the mirrors. more true, or less.

i remember every back porch i've ever sat
on clear as day. braided plastic shoulder
bones, splinters working up the courage and
that purpling sky. everything in the distance,
city, ocean, valley. no hurry. every
thing kind. be there when i get there. on the
weathered railing a coffee cup from a

vacation to the outer banks ten years ago or more, handle broken off, holds the whole year's worth of cigarette butts. i never chose to leave, not even when i needed to go. if anyone asked me to stay put i'd have done it.

1/7/2020

we put the shepherd down in january
at the beginning of the bad year,
before the virus hit new york and then chicago
and then a little town south of boston
where photo albums are collecting dust in the garage.
we put the shepherd down on a good morning—
that's the hard part—and when the lady arrived
with her long needle in its black case,
he danced down the driveway to meet her.
that bright sun. the grass would be clean for another week.
we burned him with his favorite toy and five days later
i moved to the city and a month later the virus arrived.
and the bad year has lasted longer than that, three
times as long and still counting now in another january.
we put the shepherd down and everybody was there
and my sisters and i poured whiskey and said
it was a good day, and wasn't that a good thing,
and wasn't that the hard part. i've done the math.
we may only have a month of days left together,
the weddings, the babies, no more dogs left
to put down. before the virus i wasn't thinking like that.
wasn't always trying to figure how long is left
before the ice melts, the body shutters closed,
the string holding the pins on the map together snaps.
the last time i went grocery shopping with my sisters
was december twenty-ninth, two thousand sixteen.
i'd bring the dog back just to put him down again.

Milton Keynes UK
Ingram Content Group UK Ltd.
UKHW040901301024
450479UK00005B/205